NOT ME, GOD

NOT ME GOD

Sherwood Eliot Wirt

Ronald N. Haynes Publishers, Inc.

PALM SPRINGS CALIFORNIA

NOT ME, GOD

Ronald N. Haynes Publishers, Inc.
Palm Springs, California 92263

Second Edition 1981

LIBRARY OF CONGRESS CATALOG CARD NUMBER 81–83174
ISBN 0-88021-015-X

Printed in the United States of America

Originally published by
HARPER AND ROW
1700 Montgomery St.
San Francisco, CA 94111

TO MY SON

ALEXANDER WELLS WIRT

UNITED STATES MARINE CORPS

They tell me, Lord, that when I seem
To be in speech with you,
Since but one voice is heard, it's all a dream,
One talker aping two.

Sometimes it is, yet not as they
Conceive it. Rather, I
Seek in myself the things I hoped to say,
But lo! my wells are dry.

Then, seeing me empty, you forsake
The listener's role and through
My dumb lips breathe and into utterance wake
The thoughts I never knew.

—C. S. Lewis

Preface

There is a Word that has been spoken, to which nothing will ever be added. I speak of the Word of Truth, whose limits have been fixed by God himself and have been placed under the seal of his Spirit. Yet no one who names the name of Jesus will deny that the Holy Spirit still communicates to the believer's heart in his own way. Such is the pattern given to us in the Old and New Testaments. Such is the testimony of the church, and so it shall be until the end.

What is presented in this new edition is, theologically speaking, neither revelation nor inspiration. The intent is to set forth the language of the heart. The thread of the story is fictitious and is not modeled upon any actual incidents or persons known to the author.

For over ten years I worked on these pages at odd moments. Help and encouragement came from many, including Miss Eugenia Price, Dr. Gerrit Verkuyl, Mr. Leonard Harris, and Dr. L. Nelson Bell.

I would like to acknowledge the help I received in my own prayer life from many sources: from my beloved wife, Winola; from Dr. Billy Graham and fellow members of his evangelistic team; from the Rev. Armin Gesswein and Dr. Robert Boyd Munger; and from the biography, *Rees Howells, Intercessor,* by Dr. Norman P. Grubb (Lutterworth Press), which I read in the High Sierras of California in the summer of 1954.

So let the imaginary conversation begin; and let it stay imaginary. The late C. S. Lewis once remarked to me that he had no idea how God communicated to other people—he only knew how he spoke to C. S. Lewis. I will add that no matter how fanciful these lines may appear, nothing that I have ever attempted to write has seemed to me quite so real.

S.E.W.

Poway, California

NOT ME, GOD

1

Myrna! Where are the clean towels? We have a plant conference this morning and I've had no time to prepare. What's more, the sales manager's quitting. And there's no soap in the dish. Myrna! Those kids must have spilled water on my razor blades; this one was new yesterday and it's pulling. Oh God, how can I stand another day of it?

The edge soon wears off.

How's that?

It soon wears off.

What wears off?

The edge.

Now, let's just hold on here a minute. Am I talking to myself?

You are.

Then who are you?

You will soon learn. I am a Relation.

What kind of relation? You know, this is giving me the creeps. I wonder where she keeps the aspirin.

A blood Relation.

What does that mean?

I am the sound of a going in the tops of the mulberry trees.

Myrna, would you mind stepping to the door for a moment? I nicked that mole again and it's bleeding.

She is occupied with the children.

I know what you are. I've been staying on the job so late at night that my nerve ends are inflamed, and now they're kicking up a storm of ESP. This is a psychic projection. Right?

It does not matter how you or anyone describes me. I am that I am.

What was that again? I seem to recall some such expression in the Bible. But never—never in my life have I had an affliction like this. Why should it come now?

I am answering you.

What? I asked you something?

You did.

Excuse me, but when did I ask you something?

While you were shaving.

What did I ask you?

Your words were, "Oh God, how can I stand another day of it?"

Oh, no. Someone is playing tricks with me. The place must be bugged . . . but I haven't really heard a sound, now, have I? And of course I know God does not speak with mortals . . .

You seem possessed of great knowledge.

Well, I never heard of its happening when a man was scraping lather off his face, at any rate.

The ways of communion between God and man are not limited.

Eh? Hallucinations, that's it. I'm suffering from verbal hallucinations. Probably a glandular imbalance. I remember now, I heard a sermon on the car radio. That should teach me to listen to that station. Myrna! I'm getting out on that golf course tomorrow and shaping up if it kills me. This is terrible. I never should have given that blood last week.

Nothing is wrong with you.

That's what you think! Myrna! Is breakfast ready? I'm not sure I can eat. There must be something wrong with my head. I'd blame the aspirin, but I never did find it.

2

Oh, no, not you.

Yes.

Why don't you leave me alone? What have I done to you? Are you trying to drive me straight into a padded cell?

You are distraught.

Well, how would you like to be shadowed by the FBI of Outer Space?

There is no need for alarm. You are not being shadowed.

No need for alarm? I go for weeks without a drink, and stop in here for just one, and zing! We're off. I mean, I'm talking to myself. Did you hear that? Talking to myself. I'm sure that's all there is to it.

You sound unconvinced.

Well, I don't want to hear any more discussion about the mulberry trees. Whatever you may be, I say you are not coming from the trees, or from the rocks, or from the clouds. I never was a man for spooks. You are coming from *inside,* do you hear? What's going on, is going on inside me! No thunderbolts. No supernatural sky-openings. Everything rational and psychological. So when you talk to me, your voice is really my voice. Admitted?

I am the voice of many waters.

There you go again. "The voice of many waters." What

is an ordinary citizen supposed to do with that? Wash yourself out of my hair, please. I have other things to think about —important things.

What you think concerns me.

I don't know what you are, or why you have suddenly taken all this interest in me, but let me make it clear once and for all: I am not interested. And if you don't mind, I would like to watch this next fight.

Your trumpet gives an uncertain sound.

What do you mean? How do I sound?

Miserable.

Miserable? Look, mine are the everyday problems of a family man who is living beyond his salary. No one can do a thing about it. If I get more money, I'll spend more, and be worse off than ever. So let's forget it. If I want to be miserable, that's my business.

I am with you.

You are with me? I told you, this is an interior monologue as far as I am concerned. Your voice is my voice. You say what I say, only you say it differently.

Are you so sure?

It has to be that way. Suppose it weren't—what would Fred Hoyle and the astronomers say? Suppose you really were a voice breaking through from the outside—Abraham, or Socrates, or Mahatma Gandhi? It would mean that the mainspring of the universe was broken. We would burn to a crisp . . . I'm getting out of here. They are beginning to notice me.

It is your imagination.

Imagination! I'll say it is. Maybe you've got that man behind the bar working for you. "You?" I wonder . . .

3

Now I've come to this room to settle a few things with you. I don't want any more of these awkward interruptions taking place while I'm putting through telephone calls or carrying on office conversations. I'm in a very rough spot, and it's embarrassing.

Then stop them.

How?

If it is only yourself talking to yourself, put an end to them.

I've tried that. I just might need a little help.

Help from whom?

There are a lot of things about human nature that the experts don't understand. I've been thinking I must be one of those odd people with an unconscious that bubbles to the surface. Low threshold type. For all I know, you could be my "id."

So you will visit a psychiatrist.

Not if I can avoid it, you can bet. The way I look at it, the basic problem is identification. I've got to be sure who you are.

I am which is, and which was, and which is to come.

But you see I can't accept that. My religious parents would have said it was blasphemy. I am personally unable to believe that God—if there is a God—would speak to me; or that I would be able to understand him if he did.

You believe that the one who made man is unable to communicate with him.

I would say so.

And that prayer is of no avail.

I wouldn't go quite that far. I suspect that many people get something out of prayer or they wouldn't keep on with it. It seems to make them feel better.

You prayed.

Oh, very hard—once. Why, I can remember memorizing more Bible verses than anyone in our Sunday School class.

True.

You may know what put a stop to it. Someone turned me in for swearing, so they gave the prize to a girl.

Yes.

That finished me with the church, I can tell you.

So you imagined.

I say it did, and I say you are in my hair, and furthermore I'm tired of being plural. Let's get down to business. As I see it, you must have some reason for continuing this discussion. So I'm here to appease the gods and buy you off.

You would make an offer?

I would, except that I still don't know who you are or what you want. So how can I make an offer?

But are you not talking to yourself?

I tell you I am not sure! I ask to be left alone. You apparently don't wish to leave me alone. I thought that after eighteen holes, you would disappear like a genie into a bottle. But you didn't, and here we are.

You will meet me again. In the morning.

4

I HAVE often thought that this room off the garage would make an excellent hideout if a person wanted to be alone. However, I'm running out of excuses to Myrna about getting up early, and I don't want to frighten Susie and Arthur. So let's have at it once more, shall we?

You are free to speak.

I have really nothing to say, except that I'm ready to make a deal.

What do you propose?

Well, I've reformed, for one thing. I've decided never to touch another drop. And I'll go to church Sunday. That's pretty good, now, isn't it?

These are not your problems.

Problems? You have no idea of my problems. The stuff that has piled up at the office since the crisis—well, it's unbelievable. My friends would say I might better be having a checkup.

That will not help either.

Then I give up. What's the game?

You will listen?

Yes.

You are certain.

Quite.

Then answer: Who am I?

I don't know. I wish I did. My state of being right now is confused alarm and alarmed confusion. But I am listening to you.

Very well. Our conversation is to be established on a different foundation.

What kind of foundation?

You are to talk to me as you would to your Heavenly Father.

That will be extremely difficult. If I were back in Sunday School—or saying baby prayers at bedtime—but all that is long gone. How does a *man* talk to his Heavenly Father?

The ways are as many as the sands of the seashore. Yet each prayer is heard, and answered.

[19]

You are serious?

To be sure. Why?

It's awkward to explain, really. You see, the people I listen to just don't think that way today. God is—you might say—moving out of the picture. We just don't feel the need for him as our forefathers did. Look at my father and mother, for instance—nice, religious people. They tried, oh, they tried! They dragged us boys to church year after year. But I guess you could say that now we've grown up. We're more practical. People are beginning to put more faith in computers. What I mean is that we feel God does not speak to men directly any more. Perhaps in the days of the Bible he did; I will not say.

Then you are left with verbal hallucinations.

Do you mean there is no alternative?

You have said it.

Well, I would hardly care to keep up this double-talk. There ought to be some . . . What do you want? Am I expected to pretend something that I don't believe at all?

To exercise faith is not to pretend. People do it every day.

Then their Christianity is a sham. A fake.

What did I ask?

You said to talk to you as I would to my Heavenly Father.

Exactly.

I'm perspiring all over. Either I am being brainwashed or I am completely losing my mind. No other way?

None.

When do I start?

Tomorrow morning. Come with faith—and imagination.

5

ALL right, then—what am I to call you?

You may call me Father.

That's odd. Only last night I read in the paper that people aren't supposed to talk about the Father any more. Seems it's old-fashioned. It humanizes you too much. We're supposed to speak of the "Ground of our Being," I think—something like that.

Men have given me many names, son You may call me Father.

I'm trying to go along with this, but I have a funny feeling that you are laying hands on the wrong man . . . that the Master Computer dropped a digit somewhere.

Why, son?

Because I'm not the religious type.

I am not looking for religious types. I look for men.

To do what?

To be my men. To accomplish my work.

Sad to say, I'm overworked now. That's my life: work and more work.

It will be different. You need preparing.

What kind of preparing?

You are to set your house in order.

Are you sure you shouldn't be looking somewhere else? The way I read your job specifications, I don't fit at all. I don't mean to back out, it's just . . .

I am familiar with reluctance.

Yes. Well, I suppose one can't reverse the planets in their orbits, can one? Tell me what I am expected to do.

You have a Bible.

I brought my daughter Susie's. I don't know where mine is.

Begin to read the passages she has underlined.

Well, here's one in the Psalms: "There is none that doeth good, no, not one." That must have been written about the plant where I work.

It was written about you. Continue to read.

"The heart is deceitful above all things, and desperately wicked." I'll go along with that, but I wouldn't say it was exactly inspiring.

You do not need inspiration, my son. You need to face reality.

No, I'll tell you what I need: I need a new job. That place has become a cul-de-sac. The management has deteriorated, and now the government is moving in. I give the situation one week before the lid blows off.

I am here to help you. You must follow carefully what I am saying.

Yes, sir.

The underlined passages in your daughter's Bible will teach you what you are. You will see yourself with the eyes of truth.

I understand what you're driving at, but I still think I have a few redeeming qualities about me.

They are not able to redeem you.

What I mean is, I have my good points.

I do not speak of points, but of life.

Sure. Well—

Study these words. There is life in them, though it may appear to be death. And meet me here tomorrow.

Yes, Father.

6

ALL right, here I am, ready to be worked on.

I am glad.

I may as well tell you that I'm in an ugly mood because I suspect what is coming. You want my soul saved and my soul is quite pleased with the way things are right now.

Then why are you so desperate? Why are you looking for another position? Why are your hands shaking?

You are mixing things up.

No. Face the truth, son.

So I am a wicked person, then, according to you.

You have sinned.

I also happen to be a member of the church—at least I think I am.

I pity your church.

My annual donation seems to be acceptable enough.

We will not discuss your princely generosity.

I don't claim to be simon pure. I never did. I'm not certain I would want to be pure if I could be.

That is true. Men love darkness rather than light because their deeds are evil.

I learned that verse once. It's in something. But the way I look at it, none of us is all perfection or all wickedness; there are just varying shades of in-between. That's why I can't accept the church's philosophy. To say that all men are sinners and that there is no distinction between them is just not true. There are lots of differences.

Not at the cross.

At the cross? What is the cross?

It is a sentence of death. The instinct that led you to the

bottle is a true instinct, for you are a doomed man.
You keep bringing the argument back to me.
You are the issue.
Why?
Because I have chosen you.
Chosen me to do what?
The one thing you cannot do.
What is that?
You must be born again.
If I can't do it, why do you ask me to do it?
Because I am going to do it for you.
I'm lost.
Yes.
I mean, I don't follow you.
There is a meeting at church tonight. I want you to go.
Church? In the middle of the week?
Yes. And take your daughter's Bible with you.
This is going too far.
No, son. Just far enough.

7

You are early, son.
I couldn't sleep.
How do you feel?
I don't know. It's—I can't figure it out.
That is not surprising.
What happened to me, Father? Everything seems to have a
queer cast. Was I drugged?
No. It was nothing unusual. It takes place every day.

What does?

What happened to you.

Father, tell me what I did. I have the weirdest memory of last night.

You joined the seven spirits and the four living creatures.

I did what?

You received a new name on your forehead.

On my forehead?

Yes. And I gave into your possession a white stone with a secret word inscribed upon it.

Is this a foreign language?

Not at all. Last night you made a decision that altered your status as a human being.

Why? What was I? What am I?

You were someone headed for personal disaster. Since last night you have become a man in the process of being restored to normal manhood.

Well, it's going to seem good to feel natural, after this.

Not "natural," son. "Normal."

Is there a difference?

Your "natural" self was annihilated last night. You are now a new man.

You mean I'm dead?

No. For the first time you are fully alive.

I remember spending an hour in a dull meeting at a church that was about one-tenth filled.

Quite true. Yet what happened to you there was something that the most versatile minds of your history have longed for but never found. Something that kings would have sold empires to gain. What you received has made you richer than all the minerals in the Milky Way, and it has brought nothing but joy and goodness and beauty to man.

What did I receive?

Grace.

Grace?

Yes.

Never heard of it, so far as I can remember. Is it something you wear?

Forever.

It beats me. I don't know anything about it. I don't even remember what they were talking about last night.

You understood enough.

How can you say that?

You asked my forgiveness.

I recall puzzling over some doubts.

I do not speak of your mental processes.

And I thought the place was stuffy and that the minister's voice had an annoying quality to it.

Nor of your feelings.

And I was trapped at the offering with nothing but a five-dollar bill in my pocket.

Nor of your works.

What are you speaking of, Father?

I am speaking of your response to my beloved Son.

Now it's coming back. It was like a Vacation Bible School I went to as a boy. I remember the big Bible verses printed on charts, and the children singing, and the teacher smiling. She told us to "give our hearts to Jesus," and I wanted to, but never did. Last night something caught at me and said, "Why don't you?" And so I just did! It's hard to put into words. It was like being what they call "under conviction," I guess, and then somehow I just—well, I just came free. A little late, but . . .

Welcome, my son.

8

GOOD morning, Father.

Good morning, son.

It seems easy now to call you Father.

It is the easiest thing there is, and the hardest.

When I think of the time I gave you! But really, I had no idea you were around like this. If I thought of you at all, it was to spot you about a million light-years away.

A father likes to be with his children.

Now tell me why you spoke to me in all that mysterious language. Were you just trying to shake me up?

You will learn, my son. My Spirit will open the Scriptures to you, and you will discover truth that you do not now perceive.

All right, then you can tell me right now about myself? What has happened to me?

You have heard the Good News. As you study the inspired books, and worship in your church, you will learn what this means.

May I confess something, Father?

What, my son?

Right now the only thing that seems to matter is that I used to be completely unaware of your existence, and now you're the most important thing in my life. I feel as if I had somehow pole-vaulted right into Heaven.

That is an unfortunate choice of words, son.

Why?

Because I am not a "thing" and because no one vaults his way into my heart. What you received is Grace.

I still don't understand that word.

Grace is the love that I show for you, my son. It is what I do for you, what I have done, and what I purpose to do.

But didn't I do anything? Not one measly thing? You said yourself I made a decision.

You did. In that church, when no one else knew what was happening, you reached out your hand and took what I offered.

You mean that what I did, you did first. I'll buy that. I saw it underlined in Susie's Bible: "You have not chosen me, but I have chosen you."

Yes. You will learn that lesson many times.

That is Grace?

Yes. It is favor unmerited by you, gladly given by me.

And it's not just something I made up? This is not some illusion? You've about got me sold, Father, and I've got to know if it's real. You're not dead, as some are trying to tell us, are you?

To the blind, son, all eyes are sightless.

I see. I think I do, anyway. Well, thank you, Father.

9

I was wondering, Father—

Yes, son?

I opened my mouth in church last night and you know what happened? In popped both feet, shoes, sox—the works.

You were thinking about yourself.

Well, I'm not bothered about that. The church has struggled on without me before. But what I can't straighten out is how we hit it off so well here, without any hesitation.

My Spirit is praying in you.

Is that it? So when I talk to you, that is Grace too?

Yes.

Of course if you were going to be technical and count things like my cussing in the bathroom, you could say that I have been praying to you for years. But I certainly never got into a two-way deal like this before.

It was not time. You were not ready. And—you were not trying.

I'm not trying now.

That is also true. First you must try, until you realize that trying is useless. When you cease, I begin.

It seems as if you delight in doing things just the opposite from the way we do them.

I do.

Do you know how it makes me feel? As if I have just landed on another planet, where all the rules are different, and everything is new and strange.

You are on holy ground, son. It will become familiar ground.

I'm not sure I want it to become familiar. Lots of things that are familiar I would just as soon wash down the drain. Here I am kneeling and feeling as if I were ten feet tall.

That is good. I measure a man from the knees upward.

Why did you single me out for Grace, or whatever it is? Do you have a special word to give me? Some tremendous task or mission you wish me to perform?

I have many words for you, son, but you cannot bear them now. This morning is set apart just for fellowship.

I have never felt you so close to me, not even as a Sunday School boy. I did love you then, didn't I, Father? In a sort of way, I mean?

In a way. But even when you put me out of your life, I loved you.

How did I get back?

You were ready. You were desperate.

Did I pray?

Not like this, my son.

No, not like this. Why, I want to stand up and shout like a cheerleader. I don't ever want to leave here. What are you going to do with me, Father? I can't stay forever at this pitch, somewhere between Cloud Nine and Seventh Heaven.

You are a neglected field. You require plowing and cultivating.

Yes, Father.

In the morning I will meet you.

Thank you.

10

Is that you, Father?

Yes, son.

Things have been really boiling up at the plant, and I panicked a while ago. Got to thinking you were a phony—a first sign that I was falling apart.

You may be at peace.

Not me, sir. You've got me too keyed up. I've been on a straight hallelujah diet for five days, and now the reaction is setting in.

What is bothering you?

I have always been suspicious of mystics. And I don't particularly want to become a mystic now.

You do not need to. What do you wish to become?

Can't think of anything at the moment. I'd just like to stay here with the Word and listen to you. Maybe I'll learn how to live.

That does not sound like a reaction.

Because we are in communication. But let me get in the car and turn the key, and right away I'll get qualms. I'll get to thinking that it may all turn out to be a seven-day wonder that will blow up in my face. Poor guy, they'll say. Took his work too seriously. Then comes the slack jaw and the glazed eye, and I'll head for the washroom one fine day with a handful of pills, mumbling to myself.

You do not wish to become a social casualty.

I do not.

Would you like me to help you?

Yes. I'd like some proof. I looked up Gideon in the Bible, and I saw that you gave him a sign when he asked for it.

Your faith is your sign, my son.

Maybe my faith isn't very strong. Maybe it needs a booster shot.

Let us look more carefully at these qualms of yours. What is causing them?

Well, I have doubts. I read yesterday that everything that happened to me can be induced by taking an injection of mescaline or LSD.

There is an infinite gulf between truth and error, son. My words are true no matter what the state of your belief.

But where does that leave me? I may be convinced right now, but what about day after tomorrow? I might find myself staring at the wall and nothing happening.

You are to trust in fact and not in feelings. Do you wish to know why you are worried?

Well, I—

[31]

You are afraid you might be wasting your time.

I just want to be sure that you are real, Father. That's all.

Stretch forth your hand.

What?

Stretch forth your hand.

Why?

Stretch it forth.

I—here it is.

Very well. I have grasped it. Now you have your sign.

What sign?

I took your hand, did I not?

Eh?

Did I or did I not?

Why, you said you did.

Do you believe it?

I don't know. It tingles a little.

Be careful, my son. That sounds like autosuggestion. You may become a mystic.

Father, now I know! I got what I wanted.

11

WELL, here we are again, Father.

Yes. Here we are.

Isn't it great to have this time to ourselves, when we can get down to brass tacks about spiritual things? There is nothing like it, is there? I notice that no matter how rough things get, my day is different afterward.

I do not wish to talk with you about spiritual things, son. I wish to talk about material things.

What is it this time, Sir?

Money.

Money? My money?

No. My money.

Oh, I get it. Everything belongs to you in the final analysis. Is that it?

You are begging the question, son.

I guess you will have to spell out what you mean. I don't particularly like to spend my prayer time talking about money. After you take out taxes and time payments, I don't have enough of it to make much difference. And what I do have, I watch pretty closely.

You watch it too closely.

Do you want me to throw it all away? Scatter it from an airplane?

That has not been suggested. Remember, it belongs to me.

All right, it is your money and you want some of it back—the biblical portion. Is that right, Father? You are implying tha███████been robbing you. Well, if you want the truth, I have. And I don't know why I keep on doing it. I guess I am just naturally tightfisted, Father. I can't break my old habits.

It is time to establish authority. You are exercising sovereign rights you do not possess.

Can I be frank with you, Father?

You are.

When you talk like that I get an uncomfortably commercial feeling, as if Heaven is some kind of bank where we are supposed to buy our blessings. It's all yours anyway—why all the stripping? I am giving up this thing, disciplining that thing—what are you driving at?

I understand your problem, son.

You do? Then perhaps you had better tell me what it is.

You just do not wish to open your purse.

Oh, that.

Yes.

You think I should give more to your work?

Give what is mine.

All right, I will do it. Matter of fact, I have really wanted to see my wallet converted, but somehow . . . And that reminds me, Father. Do you pay returns on your investments?

In your case, no.

What? Why?

You just said that you had been robbing me. A robber has no trading rights.

12

Father, I have a friend on my mind this mornin̲ ̲ ̲ ̲ ̲ i have

So have I. It is you.

No, I am not getting through. I am coming to you in prayer about someone who is in need. A fellow at the plant who got himself into a mess of trouble.

You are interceding for someone.

Is that the word for it? Whatever it is, I know you can help him. You are exactly what he needs.

Intercession requires preparation, my son.

What preparation, Father? Your Word says right here that you are eager for us to offer up our requests to you.

If you are ready.

Oh, well, I am ready, as far as that goes. Am I not your servant? Did you not call me? Is not all this new life designed to win souls?

No. It is designed to win you. When you are more solidly grafted into the vine and begin to grow, you will bring forth fruit; not before.

Father, you can spend the rest of my life trying to beat me into shape. Look at the time it has taken to get me this far! And I'm floundering all over the place.

I can wait, my son.

Then what I am supposed to do if people should ask me to pray for them? Tell them I'm concentrating on myself?

You may do as you wish. What did you do in the past?

In the past no one ever asked me—as you know. And I want no more of that life. I want prayers that are answered and a life that has victory in it. I want to be like Peter and Stephen and Philip and these people in the Book of Acts I have been reading about.

Very well, my son. Go to the place of obedience, and the power they knew is yours. There will be help for your friend. There will be help for many friends. Living water will flow from you.

Father! Are you giving me a promise? This is tremendous.

It is a promise.

And this place of obedience?

You must go to the cross, my son.

Oh. Yes, the cross, of course. I hadn't thought—I guess I was thinking more about the Resurrection, and Pentecost, and how those early apostles touched people and lifted them up.

The cross, my son.

13

Good morning, Father.

Good morning, son.

Aren't these quiet moments the greatest? Man, I don't know how I ever got along without them.

Them that honor me I will honor.

Sure. I see it all now, plainly. It adds up to a beautiful equation. But how could I have missed it for so long?

There is a cost.

Father, I don't feel any cost today.

You will.

I'm ready. Test me, Father.

You are to give up one meal a week for the present.

Eh?

You heard me distinctly, son.

Why, that's fanatical, Father. I no sooner get down to business with you than off we go into something weird.

There is a time to fast and a time to eat.

What good will it do? I can't send the food to India.

India is not the issue.

Well, it's—asceticism, that's what it is. Religious starvation. I thought we got rid of all that. If I remember right, there is a verse in the Bible that goes, "The earth is the Lord's and the fulness thereof." How about that? It tells us that food and all these things are good.

You do not need to quote my Word to me.

But I don't see the point. The body needs nourishment. It needs protection against disease. Fasting is not normal, and what's more, I don't think today that anyone considers it particularly spiritual. What possible reason could you have, Father?

I want your body to be subject to my Spirit. You are to establish controls so that your physical appetites will never again dominate you as they have in the past.

Great. How can I feel devout when I am half-starved?

Wait and see. To fast for a meal is not to suffer, son.

When do I start?

Today. Now.

What should I say to people who might invite me to lunch?

Tell them you are sorry. Smile. Gird your loins.

Yes, Father. I will be sorry, all right.

How do you feel now?

To tell the truth, I feel a little hungry.

14

WHAT did you say, Father? I am having difficulty concentrating this morning.

I pitied you at that banquet last night.

Were you there? What a question; of course you were there! I wish I hadn't been.

I know.

Do you know what got me last night? It was that fellow who did all the speechmaking. He thinks he is somebody, and the minister fusses over him, but he is not a spiritual man. I can tell. I'll bet he never talks to you; yet he is the one they always call upon to represent the congregation. I can see through him as though he were wax paper.

You are a novice. You are unhappy because his position in my church is superior to yours.

Lots of people are superior to me, Father, but I am not jealous of them.

Because you do not wish their positions. Son, you are not to covet.

How are you going to work that?

You are to take up your cross. You are to stop pretending to be a spiritual giant who is free to pass judgment on the spirituality of others.

I didn't mean—

Son, I have plans to make you a channel for my Spirit and a blessing to my people.

You do?

From this day you shall be dead to every grade and rank among your fellow men. You shall seek the lowest place for yourself, day by day. You will continue to dwell in it until you would not exchange it for a throne in Heaven. You will rejoice every time that you are ignored, and every time that your name is passed by.

But Father, after all, I am only human. Isn't this a bit rough?

You will stay until it becomes smooth.

But this will tear me inside out. I was never cut out for a doormat personality. Maybe I'd better not put in for the "channel" bit. Myrna would never recognize me.

You have asserted your omniscience. Now you are claiming the gift of prophecy.

Sir, I don't know what's the matter with me.

Your wife is not your problem, son. She makes her own appointments with me. As for the person you saw through like wax paper, he does the same. Your problem is simply you.

Father, I know it. It's just that what you are proposing is hard.

My Son will make the burden seem light.

If—if—can you really use me in this way, if—

I can use you no other way.

[38]

15

FATHER, I am frazzled. Bushed. I have had it.

What is wrong, my son?

Look at me, with the day hardly begun—stomach quivering, pectoral muscle contracting, eyelids twitching. And I can't wait to get through devotions so I can get out in the traffic and start pushing again.

It is not necessary, son. I am with you, and I am in you.

People won't see you in me today, Father.

Why?

Because I don't feel the joy of the Holy Spirit. And I can't pass on to others what I don't have myself.

You like it this way, do you not?

I hate it.

Your actions speak differently, son.

What do you mean?

You appear determined to take over the church. You want to organize things, to run every committee, to operate the controls, to be the person talked about. You seem to want to center activity around yourself and take the credit. For a novice you are quite remarkable.

Father, when in the world did I want all these things?

You never said so, son. You just acted so.

But I am your servant. You know it.

My servants serve no one but me, son.

Yes, but—what can I do? Ever since you sent me back to the church, people have come and asked me to do this thing and that thing. I didn't go looking for all this responsibility. It was the church . . .

Then carry your complaints to the church.

Is it not your church?

My house is a house of prayer.

But there is so much to be done. It's a mess. No system.

Without me you can do nothing.

A man cannot be in a spirit of prayer all the time, Father. Some things are just drudgery. They have to be got out of the way.

Tarry with me, son.

How do you get out of responsibilities?

Tarry.

Father, if I—if I barricade myself each morning for half an hour with the Bible, will that get me out of this bind?

We have been through this wearisome business before, son.

I shall do nothing except as you lead me.

You will be criticized.

I know. I can't take it. But you can.

How are your nerves?

Not much better. I feel as if the ball were being passed to me.

It is.

16

WHAT are we going to talk about today, Father?

About lust.

Lust? Then you must be as sick as I am of all the present-day promiscuity and pornography and all that goes with it. And things are getting worse, Father. Worse all the time.

About your lust.

My lust? Mine? Well, I'm not perfect, but after all, I have been faithful to my wife. That's more than you can say for the fellows where I work. Some of them are really messed up.

Your lust.

I don't understand, Father. I am a man, yes. But you gave me these hormones, didn't you? I didn't ask for them. You have created beautiful things and then you have told us not to look at them. Is that what you mean by lust?

You know what I mean.

Well, I don't see why I have to take a vow. I admit I am no Victorian, if that is what you mean.

Do something about it.

Do what? I can't stop being a human being.

You cannot serve two masters, son. The problem is not your body. You have a normal body. It is your will that creates the lust.

So I have a normal body and an unnatural will, is that it?

You have a natural will that is subject to your pride. Your task is to bend it into submission to my will.

Is that suppression or repression, Father?

It is Grace. You cannot do it alone.

Then I am to ignore certain feelings I have toward certain of the opposite sex. That seems to be it, doesn't it?

You cannot ignore. But you can die to your wrong desires.

Will you send your Spirit to help me? I can't do it by myself.

My Spirit comes only to those who want him. Do you know what you want?

I yield, Father.

It is well.

I intended to yield all the time.

Your arm is too short to box with me, son. Let us waste no more time; there is a world to win.

[41]

17

FATHER!

Yes, son.

This thing isn't doing what I thought it would.

In what way?

Well, I'm not growing very much spiritually. I thought when you and I finally got together, I would really take off.

How?

Oh, I don't know. I guess I expected people would begin to see your Spirit in me.

You hoped to make an impression.

Well, you know how it is. A tree is known by its fruit. That's Scripture.

I will remind you that you do not have to tell me what Scripture is.

Father, it isn't just that I want to impress people. If I find my prayers are getting through, it seems to me that I should be telling people about it. Isn't that a witness?

It depends.

But so many complications are setting in that I am becoming confused. The first person I talked to, told me to see a doctor.

You made an unhealthy impression.

Then I found myself reacting in exactly the same old pattern to certain things around the house. I just can't get rid of the way I feel. And that makes me wonder what it is all about.

I never promised to make you good, son. I promised to make you over.

But if there is no improvement, what's the sense of it? I

want to be a strong, victorious, heart-warming, peace-making, soul-winning Christian. I want to make my life count for righteousness and truth. I want to show the world a man sold out to you.

You want to be a hero.

Is that wrong? Isn't it better than living at the bottom of a hole?

It depends.

I guess I've got you wrong, Father. I thought—

I know. You have been endeavoring to usurp my role.

But—

Get off your white horse.

You don't *want* ten-talent servants working for you?

I happen to give out the talents. You have your assignment, my son.

What is it, Father?

First of all, to be yourself.

Myself?

Yes. You have been trying to stand on your own shoulders. Come down to earth. No wonder you become discouraged.

I guess I don't know what you mean, Father.

You will.

18

FATHER!

Yes, my son.

You are aware of the problem that has arisen in our church fellowship.

I am aware.

Well, are these the workings of the devil, or are you testing our faith?

Do not be in too great a hurry to ask that question, my son.

But—

My universe does not depend on the outcome of your issue.

I know, Father, but a decision has to be reached some time. Things cannot continue as they are.

You are not to make that decision.

I am not to make it. Of course not. It is up to the church.

Nor is the church to make it. Is it not my house? I shall make the decision.

Yes, Father.

You are taking yourself much too seriously.

How, Father?

I have warned you that you are a novice, yet you are treating my house as if you were the sole owner and proprietor. You give forth your opinions without anyone's asking for them. Who gave you such liberty? Where do you derive your authority?

I have none, Father, unless it be from you.

Then stop pretending to be somebody when you are nobody. I have not established you as the sole avenue of my Grace. I can be worshiped without your directing things.

Yes, Father.

I can settle the affairs of my house without your interference.

Father, I only—

I want you close to me, son.

I fear you, Father.

You are not the first mortal I have chided. Before I want your service, I want you.

You mean, what I am before what I do?

I mean that if I cannot have you, I cannot help you.
You have my life, Father. Of course, you have my life.
You are no longer anxious?
I am not.
Yielded?
I have put it into your hands.
Meet me tomorrow.
Thank you, Father.

19

YES, Father, I am here.
You do not sound too happy about it.
Oh, I guess I'm happy enough, as far as that goes.
Something is distracting you.
Not really.
Then what is it, son?
What is what?
What is bothering you?
I just said nothing is bothering me, Father. Everything is
going as well as can be expected, considering the crisis that is
closing in at the plant. I'll soon be out on my ear.
You seem to be in a strange mood.
What is strange?
You do not seem to care about anything.
I care all right. I just don't happen to feel very spiritual
today. It has been a hard week.
I would say you had taken a ship to Tarshish.
A trip to where?
To the beach. You sound like a man on vacation.

I wish I were.

Where is this new man in Christ? This man who wanted to be a soul winner? This man who was so filled with the Holy Spirit?

It's all there, Father. I'm just coasting a little this morning. I'm tired.

Coasting? Or sleeping?

It's not that kind of tiredness, Father. You know how life is. I just can't work myself up to a fever pitch of expectancy this morning.

A fever pitch is not necessary to talk with me.

I suppose not.

The weary also come to me.

I'm not sure whether I am weary or just lazy. All I know is, I just don't feel like standing on tiptoe.

I have other children like you. They are halfhearted Christians. Their trouble is inertia. Once in a while they stir themselves into a semblance of devotion, but not often.

It seems to me I just escaped from that pit. Will I ever learn to seek you with a whole heart, Father?

You are on a dying world.

How much time do we really have, Father?

Less than you think.

Perhaps I should be out redeeming the time . . .

You need time with me first.

All right, then. I'm not ready to work and I can't coast. What do I do—spin my wheels?

That is what you have been doing.

But—

Are you ready to talk?

Yes, Father.

20

FATHER!

I am listening, son.

I am not so sure of that.

Why?

I am not doubting you. I am doubting that I am getting through to you.

I am here.

Yes, but I read in your Word that you dwell in the heights and in the depths, in light unapproachable. How can I think of reaching you? Even the thought dazzles me. There are times when I still don't believe I am your man, Father.

Why not?

Well, we've been going through Job in this Bible class Myrna and I joined, and I kind of lost you out there somewhere. I'm like Job—you overwhelm me. And I ask myself, who is being fooled here? Who is presuming to engage in a palsy sort of conversation with the framer of the universe? It's just fatuous. Crazy. I wish you would either line up somebody else for this sort of thing, or else give me a contact that I would find less—well, awesome. Less frightening.

Whom would you suggest?

Oh, someone down the line, nearer to us mortals. Like the Archangel Michael.

You wish to speak with him?

I don't know.

What would you say to him?

Nothing, really.

Then talk with me. I am your Father. There is nothing to fear.

Yes, there is. You are holy, Father. You are hidden behind

the dreadful splendor of eternity. I have no business talking with you—I ought to fall on my face.

You may fall on your face if you wish. I will raise you up.

I see. Well, I suppose we can say that is done now.

You will have to think of a better reason to withdraw from my presence.

This is a very strange kind of worship, Father. Am I really your friend?

Yes.

My doubts are very real.

What doubts?

Oh, they crop up all the time—whenever I begin to think about germs, bombs, earthquakes, and so on. To say nothing of the law of entropy, that has the universe running down like a clock.

I am still your Father.

You stick to that, don't you.

I do.

And you say we are friends.

We are.

A friend of God, like Moses. Well, that gives me courage to hope. Thank you, Father.

21

FATHER, I have news for you.

Yes, my son?

I believe that this thing is working in spite of everything.

How do you believe it is working?

I mean that your Spirit is changing things in my life. My wife noticed it.

What did she say?

She remarked that something funny was going on.

That was all?

Well, that is the way we talk at home. I don't know. I can't explain the changes. It is hard to put them into words.

For a good reason. Have you told her?

No. I wanted to ask you about it first. Would it be all right to let her in on our secret?

Wait.

Why, Father?

Because you have a habit of boasting about everything, and I do not wish you to boast about this.

But Myrna is the closest human being to me. How long before I can tell her?

Ten or fifteen years.

I ought to have quite a crust of piety by then. Really, Father, are we not being a bit selfish?

She has had you for fourteen years. I have had you exactly four months. And I must remind you that she is not out of touch with me.

But if there is spiritual growth in a man, should not his nearest of kin be told about it?

Cease talking about spiritual growth.

Excuse me—I just assumed there would be growth, after these times together.

I look for spiritual shrinkage, not spiritual growth. I bless the poor in spirit.

Well, to be sure, in that sense—

That is the only sense there is.

Then how do you explain this power I feel today, this

sense of personal victory—is not that of the Spirit?

Feelings fluctuate.

All right, it is a feeling. I had a good breakfast, so I feel spiritual. When may I expect the real thing?

When you cease looking for it.

Give it all up, then. Stop trying. Stop going after people for Christ—is that it?

No one can lead another closer to me than he stands himself.

Very well, Father. Here I stay.

Good.

22

Did you miss me, Father?

Of course I missed you, son. I love you.

I wasn't very far away.

Away at all is far away.

I ask forgiveness.

It is yours. You seem undernourished, my son.

I'm not sure I catch your meaning.

You look puny. You are not on a proper diet.

Oh, I'm healthy enough, I guess.

How much time have you spent feeding on the hidden manna?

Manna?

Searching out the promises?

You mean in the—?

Drinking from the everlasting springs?

You're talking about the Bible. Well, as I think of it, I

have been a little slack this week. I'm not sure why. Last month I was really hungry for the Word. But for one thing, I have been awfully busy lately. The investigation has begun and a lot of things are turning up that no one knew anything about. It's worse than we expected.

You need nourishment for a busy life.

May I ask you a question that has been troubling me, Father?

You may.

Why did you put all your wisdom into just one book?

Many books have my wisdom, son. You have been misinformed.

Yes, but there is something special . . .

To be sure. Only in my Word do you find the hidden manna.

The manna?

My Word is not just intellectual wisdom, son; it is spiritual food. That is why I gave it to you. My Spirit lives in you, and you sustain your life in the Spirit through the nourishment of that food.

I really didn't intend to miss reading these past couple of days.

It has been nine days. And I will tell you why you missed.

Why, Father?

Because you have had more doubts. But you have not brought these doubts to me.

All right, I'm bringing them now. You talk about spiritual food. Do you mean *all* of the Old and New Testaments?

It is my Word, for I uttered it. Why do you question it?

I don't know.

Do you question that I am speaking to you now?

That's the one thing I am sure about.

When you search the Scriptures, son, you will search for

[51]

me. The men who wrote, wrote of me. I inspired them, and they revealed me.

And when they finished . . . ?

They finished because I finished.

Then I am not to select and discard?

You will compare Scripture with Scripture, and you will search for me.

And can I believe the record? There are a lot of problems here—inerrancy, authority, inspiration.

If my Word did not have integrity, I would not have spoken it.

What about the different interpretations?

My truth is one. My Spirit will enable you to discern truth, and to speak it in love.

You make it sound so simple, Father.

I want to see your appetite come back, son.

23

FATHER! It is such a beautiful day and I really need some practical help. Haven't we about run the gamut of my sins?

Why do you ask?

I thought perhaps we could move to a subject that would be more exciting and challenging. A new job, perhaps, working for you. I hate to spend these moments poking around in cold, dead ashes.

Some of the ashes are still warm.

They are still ashes, Father. And the way I read the New Testament, the brethren did something else with their time besides going around wearing sackcloth.

I sent them to preach sin and judgment.

But Father, they also preached your salvation. My sins are forgiven, you have said so. I am saved, justified, sanctified, born again, washed, cleansed, regenerated, and baptized by the Holy Spirit. I've got it all down pat. Now, can I forget about the past? You know I have tried to make things right.

I am no longer concerned with your past sins, my son.

Then my slate is clean. Christ has the victory.

Yes.

And I am ready for Heaven.

Yes.

How soon do you suppose it will be before I come, Father?

You would not like the answer to that question. As you have just observed, it is a lovely day.

I will come whenever you say.

I am certain of that.

I mean, I will come gladly, willingly. I have had enough of earth. I want to be in Heaven with you.

Your telephone is ringing.

Let it ring. Father, you do not believe me.

I know you, son. I know your impulsive nature. I do not require your presence quite yet. You have some responsibilities to fulfill, and some tasks to complete. And I want to hear you strike a clear note.

Perhaps the Lord Jesus Christ will return today.

Perhaps.

I wish he would. I wish you would ring down the curtain on our sorry history, and move in with your Kingdom. I suppose that sounds like a death wish, but it isn't, Father. If it is anything, it is a life wish. I never meant anything more sincerely.

Are you going to let the telephone ring?

Is it more important to spend time with you or to answer the telephone?

It may be my call.

I will answer, Father.

24

FATHER.

Yes, my son.

You don't know what a relief it is when I hear your voice.

It is good to hear yours, too.

If I ever thought that I would one day call out and you wouldn't be there . . .

You need not fear. Where I am, I shall always be. It is you who will be elsewhere.

Am I going some place then? Where? When?

I did not say.

I came here to talk with you about moving, Father.

You have not already made up your mind?

Not quite.

You are certain?

Yes, I am certain.

Then speak.

You remember that telephone call that came in. It is a tremendously exciting plan, Father. There is an opportunity to go into full-time work for you. I would like to know what you think about it.

You have talked it over with Myrna?

Yes, Father.

And with your friends?

With some of my friends.

And now you have come to me.

I'll admit I'm a little late getting around to it.

You want me to place my seal upon what you have already decided to do.

That's not true, Father. You do me injustice. The issue is still in doubt.

Your lips say one thing, but your heart says another. I am listening to your heart.

What am I saying?

You are saying Go–go–go–go!

And you are telling me not to go?

If I did . . . ?

I would not go.

You would go, son. I know you. You would find a way to rationalize your acceptance.

Do you feel I am not qualified to do this work?

That is not the issue.

What is the issue?

The issue is your refusal to give me a voice in the matter. You receive an attractive offer and you assume immediately that I approve it; that I even arranged it.

Well, if you don't approve, Father, say so!

I am not saying whether I approve or not. I am saying that you have not been concerned about my approval. There is no will involved here except your own.

But I want your will for my life, not my own.

Then seek it, son. I am looking for a man to stand in the gap and make up the hedge.

And you think I sound like an opportunist.

We shall see.

25

ARE you ready to talk about this matter, son?

That is why I am here, Father.

What do you think of the offer now?

As much as I ever did. But I am not sure what you think of it.

This troubles you?

It is beginning to.

The field is new.

From what I can learn about it, I ought to be able to handle the work. It will be a challenge, and it will mean some traveling, but it ought to work out. And best of all, I will escape from that impossible situation down at the plant.

I am not satisfied.

Why, Father? What's wrong? What do you want me to do?

I want you to give it to me.

Give what to you?

The new work.

Why, of course. It's for you. You know that.

That is not what I mean. I want you to lay it at the foot of the cross.

All right, I will.

And walk away and leave it.

You'll have to explain that.

I have told you before that as my child you are to seek out the lowest places. In this work you will be sorely tempted. The biggest hurdle to overcome will be your own pride.

Oh, don't worry, Father, I can keep that under control.

I have not seen evidence of it. Before you can be commissioned to such a work, you will have to be broken.

And that is keeping you from blessing the venture?

Your pride is the only problem.

So to break my pride, I must give up the job.

That is correct.

And walk away and leave it.

Yes.

And if I do that, you will turn around and give it back to me.

I did not promise that.

Then how will I know what to do?

Do nothing.

What do you mean?

Let it alone. Let me do what is to be done.

Now you are putting on the pressure. I have to give an answer within a week.

You are to do absolutely nothing. I am taking over.

Is this going to be something to watch!

26

FATHER, I've got to speak to you.

Very well, son.

I am getting very nervous about this. It does all very well to talk, but I'm no angel, as you know. I am a practical man of affairs, and every instinct I possess tells me to call back and close this deal.

Then why do you not do so?

Because of what you said. I am to keep my hands off. Do

you know what is beginning to happen? All kinds of crazy doubts are coming into my mind. I hear someone whispering to me that taboos are part of every primitive religion; that this is sheer superstition; that I have got a perverse notion in my head and I'm not man enough or civilized enough to throw it out.

I recognize the source of that language.

To a worried man it sounds like good advice—all too plausible, in fact.

Then follow it.

Not me. I need your wisdom.

Why are you nervous, son? Because I am taking charge?

Because questions keep cropping up. Don't you want me in Christian work, Father? Opportunities like this one don't just grow on bushes.

And what is the source of the opportunities?

You mean that if I am supposed to get the job, the man will call back.

You may so interpret it.

But suppose it turns out that this was the one opening that came my way, and I fumbled it. So I spend the rest of my life mourning the chance that I missed.

I never suppose.

Well, Father, if you won't let me go after the job, you will have to show me how to wait until it comes to me.

Why assume it is coming to you?

I guess it is because I haven't given up hope yet.

And if it be not my will—?

You keep saying that, but is it really your purpose to thwart one of your children who has nothing in view except to serve you better?

I am going to issue you a warning.

Yes, Father?

If you persist in placing your will over against mine, I shall bid you seek this position with all the powers that you possess.

Is that a warning?

It is a warning.

Do you suggest that if I get this position I may regret it?

I have told you to leave it alone.

Now I am really becoming afraid.

Whose will shall you seek?

There's the phone. Yours, Father. I don't want to have anything to do with this offer.

Very well, son.

27

WELL, it's happened, Father.

Yes.

You knew all the time that young fellow would get the job.

Yes.

Did I do something wrong? Is that why you gave it to him?

Do not look back, son. Look ahead.

There's nothing to look at now. I'm going to have to quit next week anyhow, and then I'll be out of work.

Look at me.

But I had my heart set, Father. I couldn't help it—it was a beautiful prospect.

It still is, but he will need your prayers.

Who will?

He will.

I'm afraid they won't do him much good.

Why?

Because my heart is broken. Because my life lately has been one disappointment after another, and this is the worst yet, and all I've got left is spite.

You said you wanted the work so you could serve me, son.

I did, and it's true.

But I am still here. You can still serve me.

You are trying to force me into saying that all that motivated me was selfishness and selfish ambition.

You know your heart, son.

I know the way it feels right now. And it's going to keep right on feeling that way.

Just as you wish.

I am suddenly very tired, Father. So many hopes, so many sand castles smashed.

That is right. Sand.

For a while, after we started talking together, I thought it would be different. I thought I had hold of something.

You did. You are now my son.

But don't you have anything at all for me, Father?

I have myself.

I suppose I ought to sing, "Count your many blessings, name them one by one." I ought to be so very, very happy that I haven't been run over by a truck. But God, why did it have to turn out this way?

Because I have something better for you.

That rings a little hollow.

Your ears are stopped today, son.

All right. It's going to be better. Better, better, better. How do I go about getting this better stuff?

You do nothing.

[60]

That again?

I have told you the one thing you should be about.

What was that?

Pray for my servant.

Him?

Yes.

All right, Father, I'll say the words. If I don't put all the accents in the right places, you'll know why.

Do it.

28

WHERE have you been, son?

You know perfectly well where I've been.

For some time we have not talked. I want fellowship with you, son. I love you.

You want your children to eat dirt, don't you, Father? Well, I've been eating dirt.

You have mixed it with bitterness.

Sure I have. But I have to put up a pious front and pretend —oh, so hypocritically—that I didn't want that job, that he is so much more able to do an effective job than I could ever be, that I have peace in my heart when all I've got is clinkers . . .

You need not pretend, son. I would rather have you honest.

Honest! What good does it do to be honest?

You are crying.

I know. I'm feeling sorry for myself. And for my family.

I told you I had something else for you.

If you mean this new thing that has come up . . .

What is wrong with it?

Oh, nothing, I guess. I just can't get excited.

No opportunity?

I suppose it's all right. It's just that the other one was so promising, so tremendous. It was that I had always dreamed of. I was absolutely certain it was your will.

Why?

Well, I said to myself, if you want to know God's will, find out what he made you able to do. And so I checked it out and it seemed to me that all my training and interest and skill pointed toward this other work.

And then?

Then I talked to you and you started throwing doubts in my path. But that didn't stop me. I would have gone ahead anyway, I think, if the thing hadn't. broken so quickly.

I am sure you would.

I'm not really getting much guidance from these talks, am I?

You may answer that.

I'd just as soon not.

Very well. Tell me, son, where did you discover this method of finding my will?

I don't know. It just seemed to make sense.

Did you find it in the writings?

No.

And you did not find it in these talks of ours, did you?

I guess it was a . . .

Yes?

Well, I was looking for support.

I told you not to take that position.

I know. And the Word backed you up, everywhere I turned. But I wouldn't admit it.

Possibly you are beginning to understand.

Keep talking to me, Father. You seem to give me the only relief I have found in this matter.

We shall speak no more of it. What of the other offer?

I don't know. I wasn't too interested. It looked about as discouraging as the job I have now.

Let us discuss it tomorrow.

Very well, Father.

29

IT IS good to be here, Father.

Welcome, son. How do you feel?

I am still carrying the torch for that other job. I guess I always will.

We shall see.

It seems you and I don't have the companionship we were having, Father.

Why not?

Oh, all these problems keep coming up about work. I wish we could just talk. Just be together—perhaps not saying anything.

There is lots of time, son.

It's not a very good offer.

Why?

They are suggesting me for it because nobody else wants it. I'm sure of that.

Good.

I can't see anything good about it. The work is loaded with trouble. Personality clashes, uncoordinated policy, no base of support. Everything is wrong with it.

How do you know?

I have looked into it, and the more I look, the sicker I feel about that other opportunity.

It is gone.

It is gone and I am about gone. I don't know what to do with myself. Susie and Arthur say I'm so grumpy they won't even play with me.

Do you remember my telling you to seek the lowest place?

Yes, Father.

Have you been doing it?

Well . . .

How can you expect a blessing from me if you keep elbowing your way into the picture?

It must be the devil, Father.

It is your own stiff neck, son. You think you are too great and too gifted to do what everyone else has to do—make an ordinary living.

You are hitting me when I am down, Father.

No, son. You are not down. That is the problem.

You really mean it, don't you. Abasement, nothing less. And I'm not just to talk about it; you want my nose in the mud.

I want you so low that I cannot even see you.

And you think this is the perfect kind of work to bring that about. Well, I must say I agree with you. But I still do not want it.

Nobody wants the cross, son.

I can take this work, and I can bury myself in it, and get caught in all sorts of headaches and difficulties, and win myself a lot of criticism, and not produce much of anything. You can call it Christian work if you want, but it's in terrible shape. And to be frank, I can't see that it is going to make me a less obnoxious person. I can't see that it is going to build character in me, or give me a radiant witness, or make me a saint.

Leave that to me.

I mean, I just don't think it's worth it.

If you go, you will go there with nothing but me.

And what will you do, Father?

Wait and see.

30

Every time I think about last night I begin to laugh, Father.

You are wise to do so.

But I can't help it. I think of all that resistance I have been putting up, and the way you have patiently gone on bearing it all, listening to my ridiculous arguing and at the same time paying no attention to it . . .

I know you well. You are my child.

Precisely. You let me think I can do whatever I please, and all the time I am working out the dates on your astronomical clock.

I stay behind the scenes.

But you keep moving the scenes you are behind.

I do not wish you to forget me.

But I do keep forgetting—until you tip me upside down so that the blood gets to my brain.

Your witness was becoming weaker, son. You needed reviving.

Well, I got it, tears and all, at the service last night. Glory, hallelujah. I really didn't think I would have to be put through the wringer quite so completely.

It is good to be thorough.

I was so irritated with that preacher for being long-winded! I wanted him to wrap up his sermon so I could get out of there. But he just kept going over and over the same points.

That is the Gospel, son.

I was fed up with brooding on my own troubles, and I ran out of everything else to think about, so I began thinking of the way I had treated you. That did it.

I am glad you have come to yourself, child.

It's amazing. Last night was almost like a foretaste of Heaven.

I heard you singing this morning.

Yes, the song has come back. And all those great opportunities have flown out the window.

Let them go.

Let them go? I never had them, Father.

True.

So nothing has changed. Only I feel better, somehow.

Your attitude has changed.

And I have the lovely taste of ashes in my mouth. That's what makes me laugh. The Fox of Heaven!

Stay close, son.

Bless you, Father.

31

You can see I am having some trouble collecting my thoughts, Father.

I expect you are, son.

I am still a little punch-drunk from yesterday.

You carried yourself well in the interview.

You are trying to buck me up. You know it was an absolutely humiliating experience.

You needed it.

No doubt, but I prefer to get it from you, not from some insulting mortal. Why, I have never been talked to so patronizingly in my life. You seemed a million miles away.

I was right there.

This type, this so-called churchman—do you have many like him, Father?

A few.

I hope for your sake they don't cluster. Why is it, Father, that an offensive personality so often gets in the way when a man sets out to do something? I was in a good mood when I went in. I felt that I was in agreement with your will, and I still had the taste of ashes in my mouth. I was quite prepared to be humble. It's a good thing I was.

It would be better, son, if you did not speak too much of your humility. Leave that to someone else—if you can find someone else.

How else can I describe what happened? It seemed clear to me that you wanted me to interview that man.

You have been stubborn about it.

Well, suppose I had gone to see him with all the belligerence and bitterness I had when that other opening fell through. It was a good thing I didn't; he might have got his nose punched!

I have told you before, son, I never suppose.

You do have a time with us mortals, don't you, Father! I sometimes ask myself why you bother. Why do you tolerate all the unpleasant incompetents who make the earth's surface such a tiresome place?

You are off-target again, son.

What is the target, then?

It is you. This man you do not like is your test. If you can get past him, there will be another test. I purpose one thing, as you ought to know by now.

What is that?

To mold you into usable shape. Is that clear?

Yes, except that I don't quite see why so much attention should be paid to me. Why not ease off just a bit, Father, and concentrate on some of these people I have to put up with? Wouldn't it be more sensible to straighten some of them out?

There is no way to obtain pure metal except through the refining fire.

Well, here goes.

32

Well, Father, we said good-by down at the plant yesterday.

They were sorry to see you go.

Sorry in more ways than one. But they were nice about it. I felt like a rat leaving a burning ship—and what I'm getting into now, who knows? I trust you do.

Stir up your faith, son. All is well.

I do believe this is what you want me to do.

It is.

I wish I could see my way clear to being enthusiastic about it, but the problems I saw earlier are still there; if anything, they have grown bigger. And that interview certainly didn't help any.

There is one thing about the work you should know.

What is it, Father?

I will be with you in it.

Thank you, Sir. Could you explain that a bit?

If you had been given the other position that you wanted so much, I would not have been with you in it.

You mean I would have gone it alone. Bucked the drag of the whole universe, so to speak.

So to speak.

Then being with me means that you will be undertaking for me—that I am really going to get some help?

I am undertaking for you now.

I would like to know that tomorrow morning when the first test comes around. I would like to feel that I am gripped by the sheath of faith.

The feeling is nothing, son. I am speaking of the fact. I am by you and with you, and I am in you.

And going before me?

And going before you.

I read an old Irish prayer the other day in our church bulletin. It said, "Christ with me, Christ before me, Christ behind me, Christ beneath me, Christ above me, Christ on my right, Christ on my left, Christ where I lie, Christ where I sit, Christ in every eye that sees me, Christ in every ear that hears me." Will it be like that?

Yes, son. Like the old Irish prayer.

Thank you, Father.

33

And how are you today, son?

Down again.

So I see.

It doesn't seem to matter where I work. Trouble is just an occupational disease with me. I probably ought to go on a kick of "mood-lifter" pills or something.

No.

Well, after all, Father! To spend one day at work and come home completely discouraged . . .

Steady, my son. Today is a new day.

I'm not particularly discouraged by the work, Father. It's the people. I've been meeting a lot of fine church people the last few months, but some of these types I am thrown in with now appear to be nothing more than holy scarecrows and well-meaning busybodies. I'm still new at this business, and I shouldn't say anything, but it seems to me they spend most of their time trading on their piety and abusing those who are under them. Then they gather to have "devotions" and talk about "love." Good grief.

Be slow to criticize, son. There is a difference between your suffering and my long-suffering.

But do you have to put up with people who brag about their churchmanship but turn out to be plain mean?

You have a mean streak in yourself.

In me?

Yes.

Are you suggesting that the things I dislike in other people are the faults you see in me?

You have said it.

That means I stand under the same judgment.

Your mercurial feelings lead you to make unwise comments about your brethren.

I know I got off on the wrong foot yesterday. Too many people took me aside and explained to me about other people. I didn't like the way the organization was set up. I still don't.

You may have an opportunity to do something about it.

How? I am not you, Father.

No, but I am in you.

How do I start?

By these things shall all men know you are my disciple, if you have love. Do as you have been commanded.

I—

Stop talking about it, and start putting it to use.

In what way?

There is only one way. Go and become a fool for my sake.

34

FATHER, I cannot serve you in this job.

Why do you say that, son?

Because it is a dismal, insignificant, confusing, exacting, mean job, just as I expected it to be. I can't even keep my disposition, let alone make a witness for you.

You are feeling sorry for yourself.

You can say that, but you forget I am a man and not an insect.

I do not forget.

Well, these people I work with certainly forget—if they

ever knew it in the first place. Really, Father, my position is becoming ridiculous. I am being treated as if I were a kind of lackey. They ask me to do impossible things.

Such as washing feet?

Father, your Son was a man every inch. I am too. I don't have to put up with this kind of treatment.

You are deliberately misconstruing the Gospel. You are saying that you do not wish to put up with it.

Father, if you want us to serve you, why do you permit conditions to become so complicated that we find ourselves helpless to do anything? Right now I feel as if my hands were tied behind my back and my feet were caught in quicksand.

I am not complaining about your service, son. On the contrary, I am commending you.

What do you mean?

You did well yesterday.

Yesterday? I can't think of anything I did except to feel sorry for myself, and to think some ugly thoughts about other people.

You undervalue yourself.

I? Is it possible?

It would seem so. You led a soul to me.

No! Good heavens, that must have been the blind leading the blind. Who was it? When did it happen?

I tell you this to encourage you, son, not to feed your pride. Let your memory remain blank.

But—

It is time to go to work, son. You have my blessing.

Thank you, Father.

35

OF COURSE I remembered right away who it was, Father, as soon as I got to work.

It would be well if you could forget unpleasantnesses as easily as you forget the blessings. How do you feel now?

Naturally I feel great about it. Apparently it was that talk we had at lunch that did it. But I thought he already knew you. After all—

Yes. After all.

But he says that last night he really spoke to you for the first time.

He did.

Great. Does that mean my training period is over, in a sense, and that you will begin using me in more significant ways?

No. I would ask you something, son.

Yes, Father.

Why do you always bring the subject back to yourself?

I don't know.

You have not been an easy pupil to train.

Do you know why? It's because circumstances are always ganging up on me, Father. It must be the devil. Lately, especially, I have felt that Satan has been trying to keep me from you.

Do you imagine that you are the first of my children to undergo that experience?

I know better than that.

Very well. For twenty minutes at lunch, as you led your friend to seek me, you were a Christian.

I shouldn't mention it, Father, but according to your own Word I am a Christian forever.

For twenty minutes you were a Christian in fact as well as in name.

Well, it's just unbelievable, to have a son in Christ—and now, of all times.

I promised that I would be with you.

So you did. "When the enemy comes in like a flood, the Lord shall raise up a standard against him."

And so I shall.

But what I can't understand is, why do you let us get to the end of our tether before you reach out a hand to us?

As long as you are holding the tether, how can you take my hand?

Yet in this case I wasn't really reaching out.

You were not reaching out for yourself. You did reach out on behalf of your friend. And I was there.

You were there when I asked, even though I did not realize I was asking. That is Grace, I guess, isn't it?

Keep up the work, son.

Thank you, Father.

36

I HAVE a feeling I am not being very nice to you, Father.

Why do you say that?

Because I am sort of picking on you all the time. I make you the repository for all my complaints. All day long at work I have to button my lip in order to maintain any kind of witness to Christ, for it would be the easiest matter in the world to say the wrong thing. But around you I just unload everything.

I wish you would do more of it.

But it really isn't fair.

All my children have the privilege of bringing their trials to me.

Sometimes we wonder how you can stand all the caterwauling, Father.

You have something on your mind.

Well, I don't quite see why you would call a man in to work for yourself, and then give him such primitive tools to work with. Where I am now, things are hopeless, and I can tell you for certain that we will never make a dent. We just don't have the materials.

I have heard that complaint before.

Sometimes I wonder why you honor the church, for we Christians are so slipshod and inefficient in our methods. This is a new day, Father. This is the age of electronics. Why should we settle for dowdy surroundings and old-fashioned facilities? I am ashamed of them. I want to do a job for you the worst way, but I am just hamstrung by what I have to work with.

In other words, you would like a grant of money.

That is putting it rather harshly.

You are envious.

Now I would say that is unfair. You are placing a distorted interpretation on my remarks.

It is you who are distorting, son. I speak the truth. You can do a great work whenever you choose to begin. Why do you require tools? You have a voice.

Yes, but—

Did you need electronics to win the conversion of your friend?

No, but—

What is it you are trying to do?

You know, Father, that we are praying and working for a spiritual awakening.

Then why do you not talk to me about it? You manage to speak of everything else. I want to pour out my Spirit. What is the hindrance?

Well, that's just it—there are all these obstacles, all these things that are wrong . . .

You think you are another John the Baptist. You wish to make straight in the desert a highway for the Lord.

Yes, I guess that's what I'm trying to do.

In the desert, son, I do not need a road. Prepare yourself instead.

Yes, Father.

37

WELL, you know the news, Father. We're all leaving our families behind and going off for the weekend to pray together.

Yes.

It seems we can't get close enough to you here in the city.

Sarcasm does not become you, son.

I suppose not. But I am having no trouble talking with you here. A person doesn't really require purple clouds on a mountaintop to find your Presence.

I want no bragging from you. You need the retreat.

Why, Father?

Because you are still fighting against yourself. You spend more time arguing with me than you do in praying to me.

You are too belligerent. I enjoy controversy to a point, son; you have passed the point.

In other words, Father, you want me to pray more precisely.

You are confused as to what I want. It would be a relief to hear you repeat a psalm or sing a hymn.

Now I can feel my skin crawling. I'm sure you mean that this whole thing was a mistake. That these talks of ours are all wrong. God, don't let it be so, please! I thought they were the only part of my life that was right.

You have been too familiar. Do not cuddle to me. This is holy ground. I am your Heavenly Father; I am not your buddy.

Father, do not leave me. Do not hide your Face from me, I cannot stand it. I did not mean to be presumptuous; truly, I am thy servant. Do with me as seemeth to thee best.

I do not need to remind you where you have missed the mark. You cannot neglect my church and you had better not depreciate it. When my people go to prayer, you are to go with them. You have no special secret platform apart from them upon which you may presume to stand. You are no closer to me than any other of my children. I have conferred no special dignity upon you.

No, Father.

Go to this retreat and join with the brethren. If you have anything to say, make sure it does not concern yourself. I know your sidelong efforts to insert your piety.

Yes, Sir.

If you have tears to shed, be certain that no one sees them.

I shall make sure.

I want brokenness from you, but I do not wish it to be paraded.

[77]

It will not be.

Put a smile on your face now, and go inquire in my temple.

A smile?

Yes. Have a good weekend.

Thank you, Father.

38

How do you look back on the retreat, son?

I knew you would ask that, Father, and I have an honest answer. Every time I was able to forget myself, I got something out of it.

That was not often.

No, it wasn't. There were some good speakers, but I was preoccupied.

And the times of prayer?

I told you they would bother me, and they did.

You were too self-conscious. I did not consider that you were praying to me at all.

What was I doing?

Sharing your favorite thoughts with your colleagues.

You mean that I was putting on a show for them. And it's true. That is why I am becoming convinced that public prayer is an impossible exercise: I think you ought to abolish it. You certainly don't need it to run the solar system. If I were you, and had to listen to as much bad praying as you do, I would be tempted to do exactly the opposite of everything we ask. It would serve us right.

Why do you not improve it?

Me? Why, I'm new at it. I don't have the gift of pouring

out my innermost soul as some others do. I don't erupt like a geyser every time the leader asks, "Will some of you lead in prayer?"

That is right. You sit back and ruin the meeting with your silence. You think that by being less ostentatious you are somehow becoming more holy.

I have prayed publicly, Father. You have heard me.

They were unworthy efforts, son.

I don't know how to recognize a good effort. It seems to me a man is either too garrulous or too closemouthed. Either he wears the rest of us out with his sanctimony or he throws a wet blanket over it all by refusing to take part—as I do. There is nothing in between.

Why not?

Because when we pray we are not thinking of you, Father. We are thinking about the image of discipleship we are trying to create. And that is why some of us turn to formal prayer more and more; it gets us away from being everlastingly occupied with ourselves.

Unfortunately it does not, son. But there is an answer.

Yes, Sir?

It is quite simple. When you speak to me, make sure that it is to me you are speaking, the whole time that you speak.

Like now, you mean.

Yes.

Then tell me: why do others have to listen? Why do you insist that part of our praying be public?

Because I am as interested in others as I am in you. I know that if they hear you talking with me, they will be encouraged to seek me for themselves.

I am to be a performer, then. I am to put on a show, as I said, and tell the world, "Watch me! This is the way I talk to the Heavenly Father."

If you wish to put it that way.

[79]

I would be repelled rather than attracted.

That is because you are concentrating on those who over-hear you. You have forgotten me altogether. You forget that I can hear you there as well as here.

I do want to help them, Father. Only—

Then do it.

39

I CAN'T imagine why that man came around to see me today, Father.

You seemed quite nonplused.

I thought that you had sent him especially to needle me about my praying.

He heard you at the retreat.

I know. You said yourself that there was nothing much to that.

True.

So why did he come?

Why not put your question to him?

I did, but he was vague. As you know, I am not the type to be searched out on spiritual matters.

If they cannot ask you questions, to whom will they turn?

I repeat, Father, I am not a holy joe.

You seem proud of the fact.

I do not intend to put on a pious front and boast of my relationship to you.

You are proud that you are not proud.

There must be some way out of this. I don't want people to think that I have all the answers, Father. You have not seen fit to share them with me, and I am sure that you know what you are doing.

You opened up the Word to him.

But I felt so sheepish while doing it. I kept remembering all my mistakes and failures. I wondered why I shouldn't be asking help of him—or anybody—instead of it being the other way around.

He was not interested in your failures.

Shall I then just pretend that I am a tremendous fountain of spiritual truth, and let it pour out?

He is not interested in you, he is interested in me. Point him to me.

And how do I do that?

Keep yourself and your experiences out of the conversation. Concentrate on his needs and the way he can be helped to meet those needs. And let him do the talking.

If he does the talking, where do I come in with the help?

Ask him to pray with you. That is what he wants, or he would not have come to see you.

I did pray, Father.

It was an afterthought. Next time make it central.

Yes, Sir.

40

Good morning, Father.

Good morning, son.

I love you very much, Father. I guess you know that.

Say it often, son.

There are times when I am a little pushed out of shape by

the world, the flesh, and the devil, but always I love you, Father.

This is a good day, then.

It's starting out right. I've decided to quit bewailing my lot and to start thinking constructive things. It's not my nature, I admit—

Your old nature.

My old nature. So I've been thinking about that wonderful wife you gave me, Myrna, and those two wonderful kids, Susie and Arthur, and that wonderful job that is really not worth the powder to blow it up, but I'm not thinking those thoughts today, am I?

There is no irony in faith, son.

All right, sir—back to the constructive thoughts. Well, let's see. Three salesmen took me to lunch yesterday, and we had ourselves a time.

Yes.

Do you know what it reminded me of? The three men in the Book of Genesis who came to Abraham's tent—and one of them was you!

Go on.

Well, I felt like a perfect fool when they started asking me what I knew about you, and hinting that I was some kind of hidden authority. Me, the space guide to the celestial regions —when it's all I can do to put the honest change in the slot of a newspaper rack.

Are you boasting now, or being humble?

I wouldn't mind boasting, but you never give me a chance. It's as I told those fellows yesterday: how can you pretend to be a mystic when all you get from the Almighty is a fresh glass of water dashed in your face each morning?

I never chasten without a purpose, son. The vine that is unpruned bears no fruit.

That is what I'm beginning to realize. You will notice that I am not quite so eager to say to you, "Put me to the test!" as I once was. I have discovered the hard way that you will be coming around to test me soon enough.

That is true.

But it does make a difference knowing that you are aware of what comes to me. I can face the things that keep cropping up at this new job, because I sense that somehow you are sweating it out with me. And I can honestly say it never used to be that way.

You have been reading your New Testament.

And I'm also being practical. I want to keep my job and feed my family. I've tried the other escapes and solutions, Father. They just don't pay off. You are the only one who does.

Never forget it.

I will not.

41

THIS is our anniversary, Father.

Yes.

Six months ago we broke the Great Silence. Do you know what reminded me of it? I cut myself while shaving this morning.

They have been good talks, son.

A magnanimous statement. I have not been a bit nice to you.

Your company has been my pleasure.

I wish I could overlook people's behavior the way you manage to. Why do you do it?

For his sake.

For his sake?

Yes.

There is so much about our lives today that keeps on bearing his mark.

True.

What a career that was, Father. We are studying it now, you know, at our Tuesday evening class.

I know.

I just can't imagine spending six weeks without food in the Jordanian desert. And then to go to Jerusalem and be turned in by one of his own men!

That was not the worst, son.

I know it. It's almost unbearable. I can't think about it.

It is over now, son. Finished.

And I know he did it for me.

But do you grasp what you are to do for him? For now there is a course set for you to run.

I am aware of it.

It is well.

You heard, didn't you, that they want me back at the plant? Management phoned yesterday.

Yes.

The government report calls for a total reorganization, and they think I might be useful. There would be a salary increase, new retirement plan, and all that.

What will you tell them?

I don't know. What should I tell them, Father?

No man having put his hand to the plough, and looking back, is fit for the Kingdom of God.

Yes. But I'm wondering.

About what?

Our minister said we don't have to be in evangelistic or church work to serve you. He said whatever we do can be done to the glory of God. And I know there would be some tremendous opportunities to witness if I went back there.

You overlook one thing, son.

Yes, Sir?

The time is short. I have called you for a purpose. From now on, every hour of your life is to count toward it.

How can it, where I am?

Did I not put you there?

You most certainly did.

If you are faithful in little, I will make you faithful in much.

When I get to Heaven, I suppose you mean.

The times are not yours to know. Good day, son.

42

LET me see whether I am still reading you, Father: you want me here in this job—right?

Yes.

And the reason is that you are giving me training and preparation that I need for something else—right?

Yes.

I wish you could get that across to Myrna. She can't gather why I should let one good deal after another slip through my fingers.

She will.

But when? All I hear these days is, "If they want you back

at the plant, maybe you ought to go."

She is waiting for you to clarify your position.

With regard to what?

With regard to me. She will go where you go. Are you not the head of the house?

Yes—in a technical sort of way. The New Testament says I am. But I can't see any reason why I should get caught in a bind like this.

It is not your reason or your understanding that I require at the moment, son. I want your obedience.

Well, there's another thing. You would think, Father, if I were supposed to get so much practical help in this job working with church people, that there would be more Christianity in evidence.

That is part of the training.

How is it?

You are to go out and win these people, instead of hanging back and criticizing them. You are not extending yourself.

Win them! To you?

No. To yourself. Let them see my Spirit in you. Let them watch my words taking effect in your life. You are too restless; learn to be quiet. You keep wanting to move into new paths of growth, yet you are still lacking in many of the basic disciplines.

Wait a minute, Father. I was talking about the people at work, not about myself.

We shall discuss them later.

I'm not sure how this is going to work out. You know, you didn't give me a very sugary disposition when you made me. I can't turn religion on and off like a spigot. I told you before, Father, that I'm not the type.

Religion does not appeal to me, son.

What?

I want reality. To live in my Spirit is to walk in my Spirit.
What does that mean?
Your complaining will have to go.
A lot of good it ever did me. I see no problem there.
So will the hours that you waste in daydreaming.
And what do I put in their place?
You will need time with me, and in the study of my Word.
Very good. Now I'll tell you the truth, Father. I really do want to grow your way. I'm tired of my kind of growth that turns out to be forever laying foundations. If you mean that I can build with Christ, I'm interested. I might even like to become a man of prayer—if it were this kind of prayer.
We shall see.

43

Good morning, Father. Things are better.
Good.
I decided you should be the first to be told, even though you already know about it. And I know exactly what you are going to say. It is not the people who are different; I am different. But I am not so certain that it is entirely a subjective matter.
You are right, son. It is not.
The thing I notice the most is attitudes. Ever since that retreat there has been a kind of thawing toward me in some quarters. What did I say out there, I wonder?
There are other factors.
Of course. For one thing, ever since Myrna came to the

office with me that day and they got a look at her, many people have been more civil to me. And I'll admit I have tried to be more agreeable.

Yes.

I know this job will never amount to anything even if I were to stay here a hundred years. But it's just possible that I am catching on to what you had in mind in putting me here.

Tell me what you think.

That fellow you said I was able to lead to you—the one who went home and talked to you after we had lunch—remember?

Yes.

He has asked me to come out to his church to speak.

I know.

This may be a developing opportunity. I mean, perhaps others will invite me.

Perhaps.

Again I know what you are going to say: "Don't start the buildup." All right, Father, I have learned. I'll try to keep out of the way. I won't act coy and I won't go shopping for engagements.

You have your own Bible well marked now, son. Turn to Jeremiah 45.

Let's see . . . I've got it: "Seekest thou great things for thyself? Seek them not."

Let that be your Word for this morning.

Honestly though, our friend is buying a pig in a poke. He doesn't know what a terrible speaker I am.

Do not concern yourself about that, son.

Why?

If you let my Spirit fill you, he will put words in your mouth. You prepare; he will declare.

What about afterward? Because if people were to ask questions, I would not have the slightest idea how to formulate a sensible answer.

There is light for those who seek. Do you ask for wisdom?

Yes, Father.

Then you shall have it.

44

NINETY-NINE times out of a hundred I would be inflated with pride and doing my utmost to conceal it; but it isn't that way today, Father. I'm scared to death.

What did you learn when you spoke last night?

I learned that there is so much pretense in the spiritual realm, and so little actual communication with you taking place, that almost no one honestly believes it can happen. The most they will do is express a pious wish that it *ought* to happen.

I told you that I have chosen you.

Yes, but not to be a freak! You never intended anything like that for me, did you, Sir?

I did not.

Well, there were two men among those who came up to me after all my talk. One hinted that I was a liar and the other seemed more than convinced that I was a psychotic, and I wasn't able to change either opinion much.

A man who talks to me as you have talked is not being a freak. He is struggling to be normal.

You told me that once, and I was trying to put it in my own words last night. Well, some of the people seemed to believe me, anyway. Even if I was scared I was thrilled at the response afterward. I can't get it out of my mind. It looks as if a whole new world is opening up before me, Father.

What kind of world, son?

I mean the hunger in the hearts of those people was so unmistakable. They want what we have had, you and I. They have a great deal of trouble—just as I had—accepting the fact that you are real. One man said to me that the church people are sick to death of polishing their candelabra. Another told me he hadn't been able to get to you for fifteen years because of all the stuffed shirts that got in his way.

Nothing is as satanic as spiritual pride, son—but it is a sword that cuts both ways. The ostentation of the Levite is no worse than the arrogance of those who criticize him.

That doesn't leave me much room. Anyway, I see now that this is the greatest thing that has ever happened to me. I want to share it with people. Maybe my gifts are limited, but the need is there. Thanks to you, Father, we may be on our way at last.

Just this word, son: Stick to what you know. There are many questions that you will not be able to answer. You are an ignorant man. You do not know where the truth lies in many of the great issues of life. If you ever begin to pontificate, I will seal your lips. Now you have my blessing.

Thank you, Father.

I have one further word. I shall give it to you tomorrow.

I'll be waiting for it.

Good.

And Father—just in case I never mentioned it—I am so glad you spoke to me that day when I was shaving.

So am I.

And I am glad, too, that I answered—that I didn't keep you waiting at the door forever, as if you were a stranger.

No one waits at the door forever, son—not even a stranger.

[90]

45

Goᴏᴅ morning, Father.

Good morning, son. As I told you, I have something to impart to you today.

Yes, Sir?

You are not to come into this room for prayer any more.

Here? Why not?

We shall no longer be speaking quite in this way for a while.

What is it, Father? Are you leaving me?

I shall never leave you, son. But you have many things yet to comprehend. It will be a way of learning for you—and of maturing.

But why? Why this? What have I done?

You have done nothing. I do not wish you to become too attached to any abiding place on this earth.

Where will I find you, then? Where will you be?

Where men have always found me: in the Holy Scriptures, in the worship services of the church, and in the depths of the heart.

And nowhere else?

In the world. Yes, I shall be there also, son.

Won't you talk with me any more?

I will, but not just in this way—for a season.

I don't understand. You must be holding my sins against me—some new act I have committed, maybe. And just as we were really beginning to click, just as . . . I mean, why does it have to happen now, Father?

You are to go into Arabia.

I suppose I should know what that means, but I don't.

Arabia is open country, son. There are no prayer rooms off the garage.

Didn't Moses go into Arabia? And Paul? Wasn't that—let me think—wasn't that where they saw your glory?

Yes.

Does that mean, then, that I have a tremendous spiritual experience ahead of me? Is that what you are hinting at?

No, son, it is the opposite. I am telling you that you are one of my common children, and you are about to become even more so. That is what it means to be chosen.

I am to become more ordinary than the ordinary? Something like that?

Yes.

But you are not withdrawing your Spirit from me?

I am not. I am making it possible for you to see me in a new and different way—a way that is high and lifted up. Be of good cheer; it will bring you great joy.

Father!

Yes, my son.

I feel numb. I know it will pass, and you say that I will be stronger than ever, and that you will bless my labors, and all that. But God, before too long, will you come back? Will you come to this little room, so we can talk like this? Can I sound off as I used to? Will it be as it was?

Nothing is ever as it was, son. I am eternal. We shall speak again, and it will be far better than this. Meanwhile my Spirit is upon you, and you have my Word.

Father! Father! There are so many questions. Shall I see your majesty—your glory? The chariots of Israel, and the horsemen . . .

You have my Word.

Father! Wait. There's something more I forgot to ask you. It's about the Lord Jesus, when he returns . . . what . . . how

[92]

. . . so many things. Don't go yet—please—
. . . my Word . . .

46

The heavens declare the glory of God;
    and the firmament sheweth his handiwork.
Day unto day uttereth speech,
    and night unto night sheweth knowledge. . . .

The law of the Lord is perfect,
    converting the soul;

The testimony of the Lord is sure,
    making wise the simple.
The statutes of the Lord are right,
    rejoicing the heart;
The commandment of the Lord is pure,
    enlightening the eyes.

The fear of the Lord is clean,
    enduring for ever;
The judgments of the Lord are true and righteous
    altogether.
More to be desired are they than gold,
    yea, than much fine gold;
        sweeter also than honey and the honeycomb.
Moreover by them is thy servant warned;
    and in keeping of them there is great reward.

Who can understand his errors?
    Cleanse thou me from secret faults.
Keep back thy servant also from presumptuous sins;

[93]

let them not have dominion over me;
Then shall I be upright,
    and I shall be innocent from the great transgression.
Let the words of my mouth,
    and the meditation of my heart,
        be acceptable in thy sight,
O Lord,
    my strength,
        and my redeemer.

—PSALM 19